The Ultimate Inspiration and UPLIFT

By Marzette Henderson Jr.

Email: mhendersonjr32@yahoo.com

Website; mhendersonjr.com

Published by: Hyde Park Publishing.

Editor: Ayana Trice-Henderson
Cover Designer: Joe Gattone
Logo Designer: Ronald Ragland

ISBN: 978-0-615-33650-3

Acknowledgments:

I give infinite gratitude to God for being the channel/vessel for The Ultimate Inspiration and UPLIFT. Also, I would like to give infinite gratitude to my beautiful wife Ayana for all your love, help, and understanding during this mission; you are the great love of my life and have been very instrumental and dedicated in supporting me on my mission of uplift. I would also like to give the most deep thanks to my family including my mother Jacqueline Kay Henderson; Mom, I love you so much, you passed when I was only one and you were nineteen, however, this book is a direct result of you having lived and loved and without you I would not be here – this book is a testament to your life; and also my father Marzette Henderson Sr. as well as Cleotha Moss Sr., Nathaniel and Juanita Bryant, Rosie Lee Boyd and Robert White, Maua Henderson, Casarine Davis, Lawrence Moss, Gail Moss, Denise Henderson, Claudette Henderson, Marzette

A.N. Henderson, and many other family members for positively touching my life. I give the deepest gratitude to **The Most Honorable Dr. Ernest Everett Just, The Most Honorable Bishop Edgar Amos Love, The Most Honorable Dr. Oscar James Cooper,** and **The Most Honorable Professor Frank Coleman,** also known as the **Ques,** for being the channels/vessels for **Omega Psi Phi Fraternity Incorporated** and the divine principles of **Manhood, Scholarship, Perseverance,** and **Uplift.** I would also like to give deep gratitude to **Epsilon Beta Chapter** -- the Uplift chapter, including the following brothers: William Lucky, Leonardo Jones, Sterling Gant, Byron Williams, Terry Robinson, Cydney Muhammad, David Green, Jefferson Davis, Roy Shephard, David Lee, Troy Collins, Virgil Huff, Eric Smith, David Yarborough, Jabril Muhammad, Fred Johnson, Andre Small, Darrek Bramlett, Oscar Scott, Rah Ama, Allatwon Jackson, Kendall Moore, Steven Tinch, David Kenebrew, Michael Thornton Jr., and the thousands of brothers I have met that have positively affected my life including, Dr. William A. Smith, Estavon Hampton, Alphrin Norman, and Fredrick Brown, I would also like to give thanks to my in-laws Nancy Currier and John Trice and brother in-law Yohance Trice as well as motorcycle chapter Envy including founders Jelani Howard, Randall Winbush, Robert Franklin, and Moses Moreno; Two Wheels, One Love; my friends, and others I have met on this thrilling expedition. Lastly, I want to give thanks to all my ancestors and the spiritual teachers who I have had the opportunity to learn from including, The Soka Gakkai International and members Stephanie Shaw, Linda Spriggs, Master Kim of The Peace School, etc. Your insight has been priceless.

Dedication:

I AM dedicating this book to humanity reaching the highest spiritual attainment possible.

Introduction:

The purpose of this book is to inspire and uplift humanity. This is a **bold action** to cause a positive difference in the face of Mother/Goddess Earth and the consciousness of her people. Read it on a continual basis; it is designed to positively change America and the World and raise our positive vibrations. America is self-correcting and the World is positively changing. On an individual level, it will help you add to your **Perfect Divine-Human Unity**. It will also help you self-correct, awaken to full consciousness, uplift your spirit, show unconditional /non-judgmental love and infinite compassion; attain at-one-ment, Christ Consciousness or Nirvana, seek the light, be infinitely happy, walk a spiritual path; help you to manifest the Christ Force within and help you co-create the Kingdom of Heaven without; help you find your human joy, self-realize, express gratitude, attune to the Divine, make the best choices in life; achieve victory in your *dreams and goals, live in harmonic balance with all creation, release all doubt, fear, and worry; live though your higher self with unlimited enthusiasm and excitement, be your brother's and sister's keeper, express your ideal and help you believe and know and have hope and faith that God exists through you and that we as humanity are self-correcting, perfecting, and uplifting America from her place of apostasy towards recognition of her Master; and when America is uplifted, there will be a major spiritual shift in the consciousness of the World and the World will positively change. This book is bringing forth a new consciousness, a new way to positively see ourselves and the World around us. The terms New America and New World are used to reflect this new energy; a new beginning, a New Heaven and New Earth.*

Great, Mighty, and Powerful:

You can have what you are looking for, you can have what you truly want and need.

Remember, you, are great, mighty, and powerful and you have the infinite power inside you, so far, beyond your wildest dreams. Whatever you want to be, you can be; anything you want to do, you can do; you can work hard and/or smart, and if you want to be it, or do it, you can; and you are, it is happening for you right now.

∽

God is love is life.

∽

Love is the indicator from the Heavens that we are here for a purpose: to love and be loved is to be shown a peek of Heaven.

The Meaning of Life: is to give our lives meaning.

∞

We are unlimited beings. We are infinite compassion, energy, enthusiasm, excitement, fun, gratitude, happiness, harmony, healing, health, inspiration, joy, knowledge, life, light, love, meditation, motivation, playfulness, power, possibilities, prayer, sexiness, strength, success, supply, vision, wellness, and wisdom manifested in the physical form.

∞

The most significant attributes in life are compassion and knowledge, love and wisdom.

∞

Life is a training ground and school for our soul's spiritual education and because of this it is hardcore, but we can handle it.

Life:

Life is the most extraordinary blessing; pure joy, a miracle, a great gift, a legendary dream, a personal mission to give love or receive love, a wonderful game to be played, a test for our ideals, a boot camp and school for our souls spiritual instruction, a journey for humans to improve and reach perfection, and an opportunity to express our God/Goddess given individuality. It is a blessing beyond our wildest wishes of what a blessing can be.

⚭

Loving others completely, divinely, infinitely, non-judgmentally, purely, and unconditionally; as we love ourselves, is the most important thing we do in our lives.

⚭

We must look on the positive side of each and every experience.

The Fruits of the Spirit:

The fruits of the spirit are: divine love, faithfulness, gentleness, goodness, honesty, kindness, patience, peace, pure joy, and self-control. When we use them we will be richer than the person richest in material wealth.

The best things in life don't cost a thing.

❧

The thoughts we think are the thoughts of the Creator.

The words we speak are the words of the Creator.

The actions we take are the actions of the Creator.

❧

We possess free will; if we transform the way we are, then we can transform our future.

Free Will I:

The greatest gift we are blessed with is the free will to manifest our own destiny and express our most compassionate, knowledgeable, loving, powerful, wisdom filled, spiritual selves.

∞

Free Will II:

The supreme gift we are given is the free will to maximize our own energy and experience the most impressive, majestic, splendid, and magnificent version of ourselves.

∞

We manifest our version of the Kingdom of Heaven on Mother/Goddess Earth through our compassion, complete love, gifts and talents, service, and Divine-Human unity.

Karma I:

Karma is the universal law of cause and effect. We reap what we sow; we receive the energy we give out. Karma is the sum of our thoughts, words, and actions.

∞

Karma II:

Karma is the totality of our thoughts, words, and actions. The spiritual law of karma forces us to learn natural law whether we want to or not. We should work towards creating positive karma through our good thoughts, kind words, and helpful actions.

∞

The material or physical, at its best, is only temporary. The objects that we create from our spiritual desires and spiritual purposes are eternal.

Thoughts, Words, and Actions:

We are responsible for our thoughts, words, and actions. There is power in our thoughts. Thoughts are what create our experiences and we construct our environment by our thoughts. Physically, this may take awhile, but spiritually, it is immediate. We should understand the power of our thoughts, so we can watch them more closely. Our thoughts are real, the mind is the builder, and the things we think about can become misdeeds or miracles! We should also understand the tremendous power of our words, if we did, we would rather be silent than to say anything negative. A kind word brings pure joy, turns away anger, and will make the day much brighter for you. Also, a kind word will make the day brighter for others by making them more in rhythm with divine love, gentleness, goodness, hope, kindness, and patience; we create positive karma and security for ourselves in the things that take hold on harmony, honesty, love, peace, and pure joy. These qualities must always be a part of our lives. So, try in your own life experience to speak kindly to yourself and everyone else and see what kind of day and life this will create for you. Lastly, it is not what we say that counts, but who and what we are! Our actions speak louder than our words. We create our strengths and weaknesses by our thoughts, words, and actions. Our bliss begins in our own minds, souls, and bodies.

⚬

Our lives will be joyful when we decide to always have a positive influence on one another. By being positive and helpful towards one another, even at unexpected times, we can make the most out of our time spent here on Mother/Goddess Earth.

The Key:

You are the key to unlocking your highest human potential. <u>Find the spiritual practice that resonates with you</u> and use it now to manifest the true you, the you, that you are meant to be; manifest the true you, who you are, the real you.

∞

Regardless of how much we perceive life as a challenge, difficulty, disharmony, ill, pain, problem, severe hardship, suffering or trouble; remember, it is always better to have life than not.

∞

There are no accidents in God's universe.

Everything that happens in life happens for a reason.

New Inner Peace to World Peace:

A new inner peace must begin within ourselves, within our own hearts, before we apply ourselves to bring peace in our home, in our community, in our city, in our state, in our nation, and then the World.

❧

We chose to be living at this point in time, at this place, and at this moment in human history. Our own desire to grow, expand, and serve leads us to be born here in this New World. We are where we need to be. This is the precise moment to really and truly know that we can make a positive difference.

❧

Mother/Goddess Earth is similar to a school in a university in which souls attend to spiritually advance.

Gods and Goddesses:

GOD said, "You are Gods and Goddesses, you are all sons and daughters of the Most High."

❧

Opportunities:

We all enter our life experience with opportunities. The choices are always within us, within self. To tap into our infinite power, our ability to do things, and be things, and accept things, is within us; and nothing can stop us, from our destiny, our promise, our success, and our greatness.

❧

Ripples:

We send out ripples of divine love, goodness, and hope when we share a smile or assist others in some spontaneous way.

Happiness, Pure Joy, Laughter, and Smiles:

We must create an atmosphere of pure joy. Please create only infinite happiness, laughter, pure joy, and smiles. Live for the pure joy of being, even through the times that are the most difficult. We can do some of our greatest good with the talents we have by brightening where we are day to day with our smiles. Our infinite happiness will shine as bright as the sun and radiate to others. So, retain the ability to laugh; laughter is one of our greatest assets.

❧

By giving love we obtain and experience an over abundance of love from the universe. We need to love one another in order for harmony and peace to be the standard on Mother/Goddess Earth. Love is the only thing that really matters in our lives; love is joyful.

Illusions:

Do not let fear limit your opportunities. In our true nature, our spiritual nature, there are no limitations. One only limits self through doubt, fear or worry. Doubt, fear, and worry are just illusions, they are not real. As soon as we are able to meet doubt, fear or worry directly, to face them, they disappear.

∞

We are all channels/vessels for the great, divine, and infinitely loving force called God to manifest on the physical plane.

∞

By divine design severe hardships are necessary for our soul's evolution.

∞

Everyone is a mega star that shines in their own way; so, let your inner light shine.

Truth I:

Truth unfolds itself to us in stages. As we assimilate and understand a stage, the next stage is revealed for us to think over.

∞

Truth II:

Whether we are searching for truth or not, God is where all paths lead. The truth is this, all paths ultimately lead back to love -- the spirit of God.

∞

What is vital is the way we show our love for God by how we treat our brothers and sisters. What we do to others, we do to ourselves and God. Karma will do to us, what we do to others. God forgives us and loves us, and expects us to forgive and love our brothers and sisters as well.

Humans I:

Humans are great, mighty, playful, and powerful spiritual beings with the purpose of creating good things on Mother/Goddess Earth. Our good is not normally achieved in bold actions, but in small acts of kindness towards others. It is the little things that count, because they reveal the true motive behind our actions and demonstrate in a better way who and what we really are.

∞

Humans II:

Humans: great, mighty, playful, and powerful spiritual beings with a sense of purpose, self-esteem, and self-respect, incarnated in a physical form to co-create the Kingdom of Heaven on Mother/Goddess Earth.

The power of a Smile:

A simple smile has the infinite power to ignite a chain reaction of divine love, which is able to travel across the planet and positively change the path of human existence.

∞

Body by God:

Our body is: absolutely wonderful, agile, brilliant, captivating, complex, delicate, exciting, fascinating, highly responsive, intricate, multifaceted, and strong.

∞

We have the infinite power inside to manifest any dream or goal and overcome any obstacle or challenge. We are unlimited beings.

∞

Divine love is our path to Heaven and our Heaven is found inside.

GAIA I: *Parts: 1-3*

Mother/Goddess Earth has a spiritual name.
God actually named the Earth "GAIA."
GAIA is an expression of God and has a soul.
GAIA is a true living organism and has her own
energy, her own laws, her own plan, and her
own evolution. GAIA is so gorgeous and
stunning; all of us should feel a supreme love for
this beautiful planet.

GAIA is the most amazing planet in the
universe because she is designed for humans to
eternally grow, laugh, learn, live, love, and play
on her. We can control GAIA's energy through
our decisions. If we decide to live in balance
with the energy on GAIA, it is great for GAIA.
If we exploit GAIA, we harm GAIA by
negatively changing her energy structure. GAIA
is incredibly strong but has been weakened
substantially because humans have decided to
utilize GAIA's life force in a way that is
incompatible with the Laws of the Universe.
Humans have stopped living in harmonic

balance with Mother Nature. We need to and are relearning and restoring our harmonic balance and we will prosper as a race and have infinite life on GAIA forever.

GAIA II:

God's pure love is for all the inhabitants of GAIA. God is not concerned with one country getting ahead of another. God desires every person to think about every other person on GAIA, more, than their own physical. God desires each person, to love everyone else, totally, more even, than they love themselves. If someone, somewhere, on GAIA is in pain, then we should be in pain -- we must feel their hurt and we must help them. GAIA has evolved to the position where we now have the power to do this. We are globally connected by love and this makes each of us a part of one whole being. We are one nation, one people, one spirit, and one God loves us.

GAIA III:

GAIA exists for us to examine our ideals and to learn and grow from them.

∞

Faith:

God is not reliant on our belief for existence; our doubt in God's existence does not hurt God -- only us.

∞

Know that life is real and there is more to life than just surviving or just barely getting by. Know that there is more to life than just being a good person. We must prosper and be good for something, so that we may fulfill our purpose for which we are experiencing this life event.

∞

Our divine nature is super-human.

Perception:

Remember that the glass is always half-full. We should be encouraged to look on the positive side of any event, experience or person that initially looks like a disappointment or failure.

∞

Be grateful every day for the great gift of your life. Grow, laugh, learn, live, love, and play for the absolute joy of it. Have fun, the purpose of life is enjoyment. Savor the beauty of every experience completely. Play with the joyful abandon of children captivated in the pure delight of the moment. The reason for our life is pure joy and when we have spiritual understanding our physical senses are enhanced.

∞

God is everything; all there is, is GOD.

Manifest Destiny: *Parts: 1-4*

We should be encouraged to hold on to our dreams and goals; we can and will manifest them. Do not give up, do not dismay. All we need is hope and faith in our dreams and goals; our hope and faith are living things. Ask, believe, and we really will receive.

Dream big! We are already legendary dreamers and visionaries. Our dreams are the now and future of this World. Attach your dreams and goals to spiritual desires or spiritual purposes. Believe and know that infinite success will be achieved.

Whenever we have a burning desire, commitment or determination for our dreams and goals to come true, a way will be made for us. Nothing is impossible. Where there is a will there is a way. We are unstoppable.

Listen to your intuition; trust and follow your heart. Take on activities that support your dreams and goals. Do something daily towards making your dreams and goals coming true; this is the consistency that is needed. Always do your best work.

⚮

All creations on Mother/Goddess Earth possess a soul that contains a blueprint for their perfect manifestation, their perfect evolution.

⚮

Complete Love is our way to our Heaven now and in our future; love is the power of life.

⚮

To hear about love and forgiveness only -- is not sufficient. We must express the love and forgiveness we know to others. How we do this is up to us.

Transforming a "negative" into a Positive:

Please take all experiences which may seem to be a negative and transform them into a positive. Our development is improved by our motivation to take what may seem to be negative experiences and transform them into something extremely positive. When we transform this energy, we continue to grow and expand at an accelerated rate.

✤

The reason for each experience is so that we may magnify and glorify the good things in life. Good is from one source, the Living God, and has eternal life. As we magnify and glorify what is good; our higher spiritual nature, and minimize what is false; our human ego self-centered nature, we grow in grace, in knowledge, in understanding, and in wisdom, which creates Heaven on Earth.

Infinite Life:

What infinite life is all about is Mother/Goddess Earth (GAIA) will keep on spinning and we will grow, laugh, learn, live, love, and play on her forever and ever, and ever. We will live in the highest spiritual attainment possible. We will bring **Perfect Divine-Human Unity** *into our consciousness and have it stay there all the time and our connection to God will be there -- our evolved soul and spirit in one-ness with divinity -- our super conscious mind awakened. We will be consciously aware that we are infinitely powerful spiritual beings meant to create great things on GAIA. This is what our exciting journey infinite life is.*

∞

The Creator has made a promise not to get involved in our lives unless welcomed.

Knowledge: Parts: 1-4

All knowledge is given as we are prepared to receive it.

Spiritually, we vibrate at different levels of light (Aura)--which is knowledge. All knowledge should be used in a way that will give help and assistance to others and God's burning desire is for knowledge of the Creator to be manifested in the living World.

All knowledge is of and through God.

All knowledge is power.

⚭

Mission Possible:

Every soul has a definite mission to do on Mother/Goddess Earth. Every soul has chosen their mission in life and we alone must find and do our mission. Very few of us are failures in our life's mission.

Soul Food:

All experiences are food for our Soul and we require positive experiences and negative experiences in order to grow and learn. Before we can truly feel joy, we have to experience sorrow. For many of us the things that are of sorrow facilitate a greater opening of the soul and spirit. Difficult experiences help us to acquire a better understanding of ourselves so that we can make the best choices. Every experience is an opportunity for us to grow by and our growth is a process.

∞

Whatever individual success we attain in life is worthless unless we share it to benefit our brothers and sisters. The greater individual is the one who is the servant of others. We are blessed with our abilities and gifts to help us be of service, and in serving our brothers and sisters we grow spiritually.

Start the transformation you want to see:

The way we transform and create a New America and New World is to start with one person. One person transforming, and then because of this, another person will transform for the greater. The only way to transform America and the World is to start with one person (you in service). One will become a community, which will become a city, which will become a state, which will become a nation, and then the World, and so, by phases, the whole future of the human race. This is the only way to start a major positive transformation.

The only thing it takes to transform America and the World is to transform one individual (ourselves), which, in turn, will set off a chain reaction of transformation from one individual to another. Everyone is of one spirit and to transform America and the World we only have to transform ourselves.

Animals:

All animals on Mother/Goddess Earth (GAIA) help teach humans that non-judgmental and unconditional love is what is significant in our lives. When we show our respect and love for animals, we show our respect and love for God.

∞

We are accountable for our actions. All of our actions, positive or negative, can have an impact which can be felt throughout the globe and affect many people for many generations.

∞

During our lives by divine design we are exposed to severe hardships for the purpose of soul development. Suffering dissolves the human ego (the false self), and leads to our complete restoration with the divine nature within us (the Higher Self).

Perfect Love:

No soul is born evil. We were conceived in love spiritually, and love is at the center or heart of our being. It is the absence of love that distorts people. Evil does not exist; the horrible things that have happened to people might make them do evil things or people may do awful things out of ignorance and need, but their souls are not wicked. What we all seek, what sustains us, what we need, is love. Love is the divine power which creates and sustains the unity of the entire universe. Our hearts consist of love; the type of love that cures, heals, and renews us. The very heart of our being is light, life, and perfect love. Our hearts are perfect love; this love, this perfection, this God-ness, is us. This God-ness is at the heart of our being. We are all extremely beautiful creations in our hearts and just like the rest of God's universe we are implanted with the blueprint to self-correct.

The Church is within you:

There is nothing that anyone can tell us, nor that any source can give us, that can be given to us of God that can cause us to know God better than from within our own hearts. ***The Church is within us.*** The church begins in us, before we find it any building or minister, pope, preacher, priest, rabbi or reverend, it begins in self! Our bodies are without a doubt the Temple of the Living God!

 ∽

The things that we know about good must first come from within ourselves. The things that we know about God must be manifested from within. To have heard about our Creator is not to know. To apply and be and live the Creator within is to know.

 ∽

Learn how to say NO when necessary!

Soul and *Spirit:*

Our souls and spirits are immortal and eternal and there is a clear separation between the soul and spirit. The soul is the evolving portion of our divine nature. The soul is always listening, learning, changing, and growing and uses free will to explore, experiment, discover, construct, and more. The soul's ultimate purpose for existing is to be a friend to God. The soul is a true friend to God, the ultimate friend, because it has the free will to choose to be a friend or not. The spirit is the life energy that activates life. The spirit is the spark of God that is in everyone. The spirit maintains its perfection regardless of our earthly experience and speaks a universal language with more power than sound. Our divine nature is Absolute Pure Consciousness with individuality. Our divine nature is perfect love, immaculate and flawless, it is forever glorious.

Music:

Music should be a part of our soul's growth and development. Music awakens the God and Goddess inside.

ↄbↄ

The law of forgiveness says we have to forgive others and it is impossible to forgive others if we are not able to forgive ourselves.

ↄbↄ

What we think and feel emotionally will express itself in our physical body. Our thoughts create our reality, so our thoughts can have a significant impact upon our infinite health or illness. Our mind contains powerful energy for creating infinite health and infinite wellness.

ↄbↄ

Life is what we universally refer to as "God."

Pure Energy:

God is within humanity and humanity is an indivisible part of God. God is pure energy and we as humanity are pure energy; a perfect creation made in the image and likeness of God. Humanity includes both the universe and God in its human energy. Humanity and God are two parts of one whole and we must love both -- the Creator and the Created.

∞

In life, when we are trying to do something positive for ourselves or others there may be situations that appear to have challenges, obstacles or problems. In actuality, there are no challenges, obstacles or problems; there are only opportunities. All thoughts, actions, and communication about the situation must be expressed in a positive and active manner to reach the opportunity that lies within.

The *Light* and the *Darkness*: Parts: 1-4

Light: Bliss, Compassion, Contentment, Goodness, Fairness, Faithfulness, Fun, Forgiveness, Gentleness, Goodness, Grace, Happiness, Helpfulness, Honesty, Hope, Infinite Health, Infinite Wisdom, Joy, Kindness, Knowledge of the Creator, Laughter, Love, Mercy, Patience, Peace, Scholarship, Self-Control, Self-Love, Service, Truth, UPLIFT, Unselfish Living.

Darkness: addiction, anger, arrogance, chauvinism, child abuse, doubt, fear, materialism, negativity, racism, selfishness, self-hate, separatist thinking, violence, and worry.

∞

Everyone needs to continually seek the light, otherwise the darkness will devour our souls and we will be lost.

Know that the reason for which each soul enters into this life experience is to be a light to those that surround them. As we each find someone with whom to give light to, a glorious miracle starts to occur, we see God responding to our personal prayers, readying us to become the light, the solution to many others. All of our lights shine brightest when we give them to one another and God is the source of all light. Light is life itself and as we each give our light, all dark areas will be exposed and we will continue to heal America and the World by chasing away the darkness. We will also know peace and the healing within our own souls through the Great Light.

The greatest gift we are given is free will. No one has the right to take our free will away -- even God does not! We can choose to tap into the enormous power of our spirits through light-energy or dark-energy. We get power through good or bad acts in our lifetime. The light is in all things; however, it is much easier to get power from dark energies. This is why so many people have been distorted and have caused so much hurt and sorrow to others. Say yes to the beautiful light! We are all divinely connected and we know each other, we are "one family of light." All things are of the Loving Light and in the light we are one with all of creation. Life is for living and the Golden City of Light is our reward!

God is not only the light; God is in the darkness as well, but, -- God said, "Let there be light," then there was Eternal Immortal Light.

∞

Prayer and **Meditation**:

Prayer and meditation are complete communication with God, two way communication. Prayer is talking with God, meditation is listening to God.

Mother Nature:

God infinitely loves the Earth. God created this beautiful planet for us and we are to live in harmonic balance with the Earth and all her creations. All parts of Mother Nature interlink and interlock with one another. Nature exists to compensate for the lower vibration and was designed for us as human beings to access spiritual energy to help us advance. Enjoy all the beauties of Mother Nature-- enjoy the sunrise, enjoy the sunset, a moonlit night, the color of a flower, the song of a bird, the ripple of a pond--the air, land, and the water. Water is the life blood of everything and "the wind is the Earth breathing." Become one with the majesty of Mother Nature in her true form. What we do influences all the other parts of Mother Nature. Everything on Earth possesses a soul, every one of us is a blessing to the Earth and every one of us has the personal responsibility to leave her a little better than we found her. So, make your corner of the Earth a little brighter, a little cleaner, a little gentler, a little greener, a little more hopeful, a little kinder, a little more patient, a little more righteous, showing, a little more brotherly and sisterly love.

∞

Heavenly Life:

It is a life of love and a life of conducting ourselves truthfully and just in every undertaking that leads to a heavenly life.

This is not a hard life to lead.

∞

A most significant purpose for us entering into this life experience is to either teach or learn, oftentimes both. All the negative events we experience here are either for our individual learning or somebody else's.

Everything on Mother/Goddess Earth (GAIA) has its purpose. Everything adjusts to a pattern which will, in the closing stages, work out for love, fairness, and justice.

∞

Divine love is supreme and the only thing that matters is divine love. All else, our accomplishments, degrees, the wealth we acquire, the car we drive, the jewelry we possess, and the amount of material things we own, is of little significance. What we do as a profession is not important. Really, the only thing that matters is how we do what we do. And the only thing that matters is that we do what we do with divine love.

∞

There are as many paths to God as there are souls residing on Mother/Goddess Earth (GAIA).

The **Heavens** and the **Earth:**

We do not go to Heaven; we grow to Heaven through good deeds and kind words. And although our goal is to grow to the highest Heaven, our greatest goal is to leave the Heavens and bring Heaven to Earth, making Mother/Goddess Earth a better/happier place in which to live.

∽

Human consciousness is elevating to the highest spiritual attainment possible. There are no difficulties, no disappointments, no hurts, no sufferings, no troubles, and no disharmony in God's universe that sooner or later will not be transformed into harmony.

∽

The most important objective in our lives is for us to love ourselves and others non-judgmentally and unconditionally.

We are the human aspect of God. Being the human aspect of God is the most fabulous gift and blessing. It is a gift and blessing from God exceeding our wildest expectations of what a gift and blessing can be.

∾

Hardships are needed for our soul's growth. All experiences are tools for us to grow stronger by and we should count our difficulties, disappointments, mistakes, severe hardships, sufferings, and our troubles as stepping stones to know God's way better.

∾

The Creator has a mission for us. At times, we may feel we do not know what it is. However, we just need to trust and follow our hearts and we will get there. That is because our hearts know more than our head does; our head is sometimes filled with doubt.

Healing I:

Remember, all healing begins from inside. There is a healing of the emotional, mental, and physical and there is a self-correction of the spirit. When our mind, body, and spirit is in total harmony we become as perfect as a human being can become and we reinforce our capability to accomplish the mission for which we have entered into this life experience.

∞

Healing II:

We all have the innate ability to heal ourselves. We can use our desires and determination to enable this gift. All of our healing--emotional, mental, physical or spiritual, is attuning our body, each reflex of our brain power, and each cell of our body to the awareness that the Divine-Power lies within each atom of our being.

Everyone on Earth is part of the chosen.

Everyone is gifted and talented.

Everyone is intelligent.

Everyone has a bright now and a bright future.

∞

Expressing divine love and pure joy in our daily activities is the greatest service souls may give to this life experience. Divine love is really the only thing of substance. Divine love is pure joy! Our life is easy. If we are loving and kind, we will have pure joy.

∞

Anyone that has achieved anything great has had challenges and obstacles to surmount. It is not whether we stumble or fall down, it is whether we get back up and try again -- Never, ever quit or give up!

My own worst enemy:

The greatest opponent we will ever meet in battle is ourselves: the human ego and its selfish desires: the false god -- the "beast."

ॐ

Our lives and creation are proof that God exists.

ॐ

In God's great love all prayers are answered. Do not tell God how and when to answer them. God answers all prayers perfectly.

ॐ

We should not wait to get our Heaven in the afterlife. We should get to our Heaven here on Mother/Goddess Earth, in this lifetime, and in this now, because Heaven lives; and life is going to be whatever we create of it and whatever we are willing to accept of it.

Infinite Happiness: *Parts: 1-3*

Life's aim for us is happiness. Infinite happiness is a choice, a decision, a state of mind. We have the power within our mental and spiritual selves to make ourselves just as happy as we would like. No one or no-thing can take our joy unless we let them. We should act happy or blissful and we will soon find ourselves becoming that way.

We think what we desire is money, romantic love, to get out of debt, material things, or to look a certain way; but what we really desire is infinite happiness. Wealth, infinite health, and romantic love are just the prizes of being happy. First, we should be grateful for what we do have. Gratitude and happiness are vibrations that are in harmony with the Universal-Force/God. The same frequency vibrations attract one another so the vibrations of infinite gratitude and happiness are going to attract more wealth and infinite health. Because these energies are of the same vibration they are going to add more happiness and joy to our lives. We must not wait until we get the money we desire, to get out of debt or the romantic love we desire to be happy. Choose happiness and contentment now. Then, when we get that romantic love or the money we desire it will expand our happiness, creating infinite happiness.

Lastly, infinite happiness is love of something outside of oneself. Happiness will never be gained or known by loving only things within self or self's own circle of influence! So, measure your infinite happiness not only by the smile on your own face, but also by the smile you have produced on the face of someone else.

∽

We should be true to ourselves, emotionally, mentally, physically, and spiritually so the best in life can come to us and be ours.

Self-Love:

First and foremost, we must love ourselves non-judgmentally and unconditionally, and then we will be able to love our sisters and brothers and all of creation in the same way. Love is what we are all hoping to achieve for ourselves and others because we cannot truthfully love others unless we first love ourselves. Without feelings of self-love, the love we feel for others is fake. We should first learn to love from within so the love we give our sisters and brothers comes from deep inside, from self-acceptance and self love.

∞

Realize that God does listen and all prayers are answered and that you can attract what you truly desire as long as you believe and know that it has already happened and hold on to that belief and do not act outside that belief. **You can have what you are looking for; you can have what you truly desire and need.** -- *(pg.1)*

Right and *wrong:*

Please help our children and our youth understand the difference between right and wrong. Teach them: <u>Right is being kind and helping others</u>; wrong is harming another being and not helping when you can.

∞

Conscious:

The small voice from within our thoughts is the voice of God. The small voice from within that tells us to do good things comes from God. We are guided and directed to the positive knowledge and experiences that we need by this small voice from within. It is the light of perfect love within every one of us. If there is a negative voice in your thoughts, it is the human ego, (the cause of all human made earthly suffering); instead learn to listen to that positive small voice from within.

Technology:

All technology should be used in a manner that will give help and assistance to others, and God's burning desire is that technology be used to manifest the Laws of the Creator in the Promised Land.

∞

Life is designed to be tough. We must not take the easy way out by avoiding the tough parts. We have to earn the things that we receive.

∞

Listen Up:

The more we listen to others and the less we think about justifying our own opinions, the more we are able to be of help and assistance to ourselves, our families, our communities, and the world around us. We are to do more listening and learning than talking.

Service:

Service to others is the fastest way to transform America and the World. Express your love through service; demonstrate that your love is able to create a difference in others lives. Then, their love will create a difference in your life, and countless others lives. By each of us doing this and working collectively we will positively transform humanity, one soul at a time.

The greater soul is the one who is in service to others.

❧

We are sent here to love completely, have infinite life and live it plentifully, experience absolute joy, find absolute joy in the positive things we create, gain spiritual understanding and self-awareness, and to apply our free will to strengthen and amplify our lives.

Optimism:

Bring your optimism to life. We should always be positive about our now and our future and prepare ourselves for the better, instead of the worse.

∞

When we share what we have unselfishly, the universe will give us more in return. This is a universal law. We will be given everything we have prepared ourselves to receive.

∞

Living in this World is the ultimate experience for our souls. It is ultimate because Mother/Goddess Earth (GAIA) was created to accelerate our spiritual growth. The lessons we need to learn are easier for us to learn because we are incarnated in a physical form.

Creation I:

God is the creative force of the universe; God is everywhere because everything that exists is a part of God. God is expressing itself as humans and everything in creation. Creation is about God entering into the experience of life; God tries out different forms and then goes back to where God came from.

∞

Creation II:

Creation is God exploring and expanding God's nature through every way conceivable; it is an adventurous, electrifying, never ending exploration and expansion through all of creation and humanity. Through every cell, every animal, through every branch on every tree, through every strand of hair on our heads, God is exploring and expanding God's nature, the Infinite "I AM."

What is Humanity's truth?

Are we human beings having an unhappy life?

Are we spiritual beings having an exhilarating adventure?

We are not human beings having a spiritual experience. We are great, mighty, playful, and powerful spiritual beings that have left Heaven to walk Mother/Goddess Earth as humans for its amusement, delight, and pleasure; and to make Mother/Goddess Earth a better/happier place in which to live.

৵

Our love is truly real and we are all divinely connected by light and love to each other while on Mother/Goddess Earth, as a "force of one." We are unified in this one ultimate purpose: to learn the lessons of how to love one another completely.

The Choice I:

All of us are in the position of being able to be useful. Please recognize the opportunities that come up daily in our experiences with our brothers and sisters. What is our choice? Choose whatever creates divine love, faith, gentleness, goodness, harmony, hope, infinite happiness, kindness, patience, peace, and pure joy in the experience.

∞

The Choice II:

The choices we make in our lives matter deeply. Any choice we make, we must work at, and when we make a choice we should strive to do our best work. When we do our best work we grow spiritually.

∞

The Gods and Goddesses are one.

We are souls visiting and experiencing Mother/Goddess Earth, in order to advance and expand into the supreme light beings that are our true beginning and ultimate destiny.

☙

Our adversities are of our own making. Difficulties, problems, sufferings, and troubles are life's way of teaching us lessons that will not be learned otherwise. The purpose of karma is to make us learn life's lessons whether we want to or not. We should strive to learn from the difficulties, problems, sufferings, and troubles of others so we can avoid making as many of our own.

☙

Humanity is moving away from a consciousness of duality, good/bad and right/wrong, towards a consciousness of singularity -- only the good and righteous.

God and I believe that children are our now and our future:

Children are the most precious blessings in the new World. Loving, nurturing, raising, and teaching our children are our highest priorities. We should give children our attention, care, and time, they are our future.

⸎

Know this first rule: there is good and greatness in everyone and everything that has life here, including you.

⸎

We are to do unto others as we would have them do unto us; *we should treat our brothers and sisters as if they are part of our soul and spirit because they are.*

⸎

Life is about loving people -- not things.

Be fruitful and prosperous.

Be fruitful and multiply.

Be fruitful and subdue the Earth.

∞

As we continue living, we are learning, we are evolving, and our souls and spirits are moving closer to the Divine Spirit; even through our challenges, difficulties, mistakes, problems, severe hardships, and sufferings. Sometimes we may feel there is confusion in our lives; we may feel worried or in pain, but rest assured, as long as we continue living and breathing, we are growing.

∞

From a spiritual perspective there is no calamity or crisis, discord or dissonance on Mother/Goddess Earth (GAIA) that will not be corrected.

Regardless of who we are, what beliefs we hold, what religion we profess, what ethnicity we belong to, what wealth we have, what culture we subscribe to, we are all children united under one God. These superficial earthly barriers mean nothing. We are all of one soul and all living beings in the universe are intricately connected to one another. The Golden Rule is the Law of the Universe: **Do unto others as we would have them do unto us.** We are to treat our brothers and sisters as we would like to be treated.

∽

Our divine nature is one where we know goodness without evil as a point of reference.

∽

Life is a sequence of events that is repeated again and again for humans to reincarnate, improve, and become perfect.

From suffering to providence:

Suffering exists and all the suffering we do in our lives is really for our spiritual well-being. Even the most heartbreaking of human situations produces spiritual growth. An acceptance of suffering as a needed lesson can bring immediate growth and healing. Through suffering strength is gained.

∽

Life has difficulties whether we are trying to do something positive for ourselves or others. Difficulties are opportunities for growth and development. When we triumph over them we become stronger.

∽

If we care for others, God will care for us --and do a much better job of it than we are able to. Our love has to be pure -- this is the only law God has.

Divine Design:

Our lives have meaning and everything is divinely connected. We are very powerful spiritual beings and all of our actions, positive or negative, have an effect on the evolution of our souls and the evolution of souls around us because we are all a part of each other. Our actions have an effect on all parts of Mother Nature as well. All of creation interconnects, interlinks, interlocks, interrelates, interweaves, and intertwines with all other parts. What we do as humans affects all the other parts of Mother Nature and creation. We are divinely connected with all forms of life by Living Light Energy -- water, minerals, herbs, fruits, vegetables, plants, animals, rocks, our Eco System, Mother/Goddess Earth, the Sun, the Moon, the Planets, our Solar System, our Galaxy, the Darkness, the Light, and all that exists throughout eternity. All of creation, including human consciousness, is Living Light Energy vibrating as a wave and/or particle and everything is made from the light of God which is infinitely powerful, loving, and extremely intelligent. We need to understand humanity, Mother Nature, and creation so we walk closer with God.

∞

We should be true to ourselves and then we will not be false to anybody.

∞

When we give respect to the God within others, by showing them unconditional and non-judgmental love, we will discover the Kingdom of Heaven within ourselves.

∞

God feels our pain and the pain we cause humanity, animals, and the planet.

Abilities:

We have the abilities to achieve whatever we would choose to focus on, so long as we trust in the Creators grace, might, and infinite power. We have to be conscious of this in our knowledge, wisdom, and understanding. We can achieve anything. We have to know ourselves as the channel, the vessel, through which the Creator, God, may express infinite power -- in whatever our chosen activity may be.

∞

Know that your smile will bring many to your aid, while a frown will drive everyone away.

∞

*We are here to help each other to rise to the highest plane of being -- the perfect union of a human with the Divine -- **Perfect Divine-Human Unity**.*

The GODS are one:

GOD is one -- It does not matter what we refer to The Prime Creator as -- Allah, All That Is, Almighty, Alpha and OMEGA, Christ-Force, Creator, Creative-Force, Divine Creator, Divine-Force, Divine Intelligence, Divine Mind, Divine-Spirit, Elohim, Heavenly Father, God-Goddess, God-Force, God-Source, Great Spirit, I AM, I AM that I AM, Infinite Intelligence, Jah, Jehovah, Life, Lord, Love, One Universal Consciousness, Spirit-Force, Supreme Creator, Supreme Basileus, Supreme God, Ultimate Godhead, The One, Universe, Universal-Force, Universal Mind, **YHWH***(Yahweh) or whatever; they are one and the same.*

∞

Please limit the use of the word hate, we can use dislike instead. Our thoughts create our reality and we are creating a perfect world with only divine love.

All prayer is answered:

In our search for love, truth, and understanding, every path returns to the spirit of God. Truth is knowledge of life as it was, as it is, and as it shall be. God, having all truth, sees into our everlasting pasts and futures and knows our everlasting needs. Therefore, we can trust God to provide us with the blessings that will benefit us in finishing our life's mission successfully. In God's great pure love all prayer is answered according to this timeless and omniscient perspective. God answers each and every one of our prayers perfectly.

∞

The purpose for living is so that we as great, mighty, playful, and powerful spiritual beings may share our light, love, and energy to make our lives and Mother/Goddess Earth a better/happier place in which to live.

Humans are an individualized portion of an immortal spirit that has been alive forever. Life is a cycle for humans leading humanity towards perfection and humanity's soul will in due course, become perfect, just like the immortal spirit.

∽

God created the universe. God is the creative energy of the universe, boundless creative energy. All That Is--that which we call the spirit of God--is expressing itself as humans and all of creation. Humanity includes both God and the universe in its human power. Wherever humans are, God is, and just like the God-Source, we are always somewhere.

∽

Our creation was a purposeful act on the part of God and all souls return to enhance the Supreme God.

Spiritual Growth:

Spiritual growth is a soul expansion process towards an open heart; compassion, complete love, divine-self awareness, service, and **Perfect Divine-Human Unity**.

∞

We are very powerful spiritual beings. Even our small acts can have a profound effect on the lives our brothers and sisters even though we may be completely oblivious to it.

∞

Everything that exists is created from the essence of God -- the light, which is infinitely powerful, loving, and very, very intelligent.

∞

It is within us that the divine, great, and infinitely loving force named God lives. God dwells within you, God dwells within me.

Time for some Action:

We are saved by unselfish acts. The best thing we can do to make it better for ourselves is to develop our capacity to give and receive unselfish love. When we do only good acts and say kind words we will eventually get rid of bad karma and only good things will happen to us. All the good that we do for others, every one of our good acts and kind words will come back to us and bless us a hundred times, our power will be found in love. If we do bad acts and say unkind words, only bad things will happen to us. The purpose of karma is to encourage us learn life's lessons whether we desire to or not. Our only way to get around karma is to develop so much unselfish love that paying for bad karma will serve no purpose. Spontaneous and unconditional acts of love are the best acts we can do. Acts which are measured most important are those which express love in a great, pure, and unconditional way; acts which are measured to be the greatest are typically those that are done without great display, but are little, singular acts of kindness towards others. The spiritual law of karma also demands that we meet every piece of our past karmic debts and forgive those that have hurt us and seek the forgiveness of those that we have wronged as well.

All our lives are affected a certain amount by our karma. But our free will is superior to karma because with our free will, anything is possible, anything like, unselfish love.

∽

God is conscious of the thoughts of every human and God knows all of our thoughts instantly.

∽

We are all divine beings, Divine Light Beings.

Perseverance:

We can persevere through any challenge, difficulty, disharmony, ill, obstacle, pain, problem, severe hardship, suffering or trouble. It is just a matter of tapping the infinite power within. We may not be able to in our human mode, but we can in our super-human mode. We can tap into the Super-Human God-Force that lies within.

⚮

Humans are immortal beings encapsulated in a physical form and humanity's soul is destined to live forever.

⚮

Every act and experience in our lives is important. Even the act we may believe to be unimportant may be the most important act we will ever do. Every experience is capable of bringing us great awareness and love.

Pure Love I:

Let us now talk about pure love. Pure love is the message we are given from God. God is divine love in its purest form, unconditional, undeserved, unmerited, and unsolicited. God's pure love for us is not based on anything that we have achieved or anything that we own materially; we are cherished, loved, and considered precious. To be in God's presence and enjoy God's pure love we have to grow to be as God is and learn to love without judgments or conditions.

∞

Pure Love II:

Pure love is the law and the law is pure love. God's standard is pure love and pure love for God is the greatest love there is. Pure love is God's measuring rod that is used to evaluate all of our actions. Pure love is serving God and others without any selfish desires. Selfish desires are what make our acts impure. To love purely is to receive and feel an overwhelming, beautiful, preview of Heaven.

∞

Questions?:

Did we help others while we were here? What have we done with our lives? Did we do unto others as we would have them do unto us? Did we appreciate life or did we take it for granted? Did we love others as we are being loved _NOW_? Completely? Non-judgmentally? Unconditionally? Did we cherish Life or did we neglect it? How much love did we give during our lives? Did we serve humanity, nature, or creation? Did we cultivate life or did we disrespect it? How much love did we receive from others? What did we do with the precious gift of life? These are the questions of our lives.

Affirmations of Self-Mastery and Mastery of any Experience in Life:

Everything Always -- *Everything Always Goes My Way!*

I AM -- *I AM Always And In All Ways Better Than I Think I AM!*

I CAN -- *I Can Handle Anything!*

I DO -- *I Do All I Need To Do, At Any Given Moment!*

I HAVE -- *I Have The Innate Ability To Heal Myself!*

I WILL -- *I Will Do The Things I Need To Do, When I Need To Do Them!*

Everything Always, I AM, I CAN, I DO, I HAVE, I WILL -- *Use these affirmations for all experiences and/or create your own from these.*

Eternal Beings:

Spiritually, we are immortal and indestructible. We have always been alive and we will always be alive, we have infinite life. Our immortal spirit was born when the Creator, God, first thought us into existence. We were created with eternal light, infinite power, perfect love, and pure energy from the beginning of the World. We are non-physical eternal beings, pure energy manifested in its highest elevation, and this pure energy cannot be destroyed.

∞

Know that what is truly yours <u>cannot</u> be taken away from you: abilities, character, experiences, free will, knowledge of the Creator, love for others, manhood, positive karma, scholarship, self-love, womanhood, and wisdom.

True Self-Awareness:

Humanity's true self is a spirit and our spirit is one with God. We come to Earth to learn the teachings of love for the progression of our souls into conscious awareness. Self-awareness is the prayer of the heart. It is God's unconditional love for us that sends us on our exciting adventure and it is our unconditional love for God that permits us to return to God's pure love again. Heaven is our real home; we are in school here on Earth. We should honor God by improving our minds and bodies, doing good things for others, and making the most out of our opportunities. So co-create the Kingdom of Heaven on Mother/Goddess Earth and return to God in the highest Heaven with the experience, knowledge, infinite wisdom, and understanding you have gained and God will be enhanced by it. God is everything; all there ever was, is, and shall be, is the Supreme God.

Only God can judge me:

We do not have the authority or awareness to judge anybody; only God can judge perfectly. Only God knows what is in our hearts and only God knows the truth about every soul. Do not criticize unless you want to be criticized. The second we judge someone for their perceived limitations or weaknesses, we then show the same shortcomings in ourselves. Someone we might see as bad because of their race or because they are homeless or disabled, God may know as a great person. Likewise, someone we might see as good, God may know as a false prophet with an immoral heart. Only God truly knows our souls and spirits and truly sees into our hearts and minds. We only see momentary strengths and weaknesses and the physical self. Because of our vantage point we can rarely see into the hearts and minds of our brothers and sisters so we should always think well and speak well of them.

Armageddon--*The battle within everyone between our higher self and our lower self:*

Our spiritual body is in constant conflict with our physical body. Our spirit bodies are full of truth, infinite light, and perfect love; however, by divine design they battle constantly to overcome the body so they are strengthened. The Earth is a difficult battle ground where we must meet and defeat the temptations that exist here. The spiritual force is always victorious. Seek to develop a balance between the spiritual and the physical, a balance that will bless you with inner peace -- oneness with the Divine with perfect control that is free from external limitations.

∞

Everyone's success or failure affects everyone else to some extent because we are all collectively bonded as a "force of one."

Mistakes:

God knew we would make mistakes; mistakes are a part of being human. God permits us to make mistakes for the purposes of our higher education and spiritual evolution. There are no "wrong" actions; there are only actions that either increase or decrease positive spiritual growth. We come to Mother/Goddess Earth to make mistakes and there are really no mistakes in life because all experiences are ways for us to learn, love, grow, and have a human experience. Our greatest mistakes in life will one day be celebrated by us as our greatest teachers. However, if we learn from the mistakes of others we can avoid nearly all of our own.

∞

We are here to help one another reach the highest level of love -- infinite love.

Make it a personal ideal that God is your power and strength! God is your life and love! We are in the Creator -- in the Creator we live, move, breathe, and have our being!

∞

Confusion comes unless we hold on to God's one mighty purpose, divine love. Divine love outshines everything else and is the one mighty purpose that makes this Mother/Goddess Earth experience valuable.

∞

Everything in life is progressing according to a perfect and divine plan, and the final destination for every living being is to return to the Eternal Light, Absolute Source; God's Pure Love.

∞

All humans are children of the Most High God.

If fear of what others might say, fear of the future or fears from the past arise -- say this prayer with Body, Mind, Soul, and Spirit -- **Here I AM, Lord, yours! Keep me in the way you would have me go, rather than in that I might choose.**

&

Whether we are in bliss, infinite happiness, pain, pure joy, suffering or trouble; keep in mind what God said, **"I AM with you always, even until the end of the World."**

&

"Fear not -- I AM with you," *God said this should be upon our hearts and minds in order for us to become one with the Spirit-Force; that we should not worry, fear pain, severe hardship, suffering nor "death." The Creator will help us, strengthen us, and uplift us, with the right hand of righteousness.*

Spirituality and *Religion:*

The only purpose of life is spiritual growth. The religions of this world are an external path with an ideal to lead us inward towards true spirituality which is complete love, compassion, and service. All religions and faiths are equal in God's sight and they are valuable to humanity's soul evolution. All religions are paths to God. Each religion has its own beliefs, and there are similarities as well as huge differences among them. Religions have a purpose and God made variations in religion because of the different lessons everyone needs to learn. God does not care which religion a person follows. Each of us is at a different level of spiritual growth and spiritual understanding so each of us is ready for a different level of spiritual knowledge. Each faith fulfills spiritual needs that others are not able to because no one faith can fulfill all needs at every level. They are all a variation of the whole. What is important is the religion that is suitable for each soul; the best religion for your soul is the religion that moves you closest to God.

No one has the authority to condemn any faith or religion in any way. The religions or people which claim supremacy over other religions and oppress, control or exclude others, rebel against God's law to love others as we love ourselves. God says all religions are to be used in the manner that will give help and assistance to others; God's burning desire is that religion be used to manifest pure love on Earth. Love is the ultimate goal and religion is simply one means to get us there. Religion, in itself, is not vital to God, all religions are essential because there are souls who need what they teach. On these grounds, all religions are valuable in the sight of God.

All religions refer to the same God and are different ways of expressing the same God. There is one God that is worshipped through many different teachings of many different religious faiths. God is not an exclusive member of any particular church or religion. It is the churches and the religions that are members within the glory and magnificence that is God. God is not interested in one Religious group getting ahead of another and there is no chosen religion and there is no chosen person or people, we are all loved equally in God's eyes.

Religion is used as a foundation to further knowledge. People in one religion may not have a complete understanding of God's Gospel and may never while in that religion. As a soul elevates their level of understanding about God and their own eternal growth, they may feel stagnated with the teachings of their current faith and look for a different religion or philosophy to fill that longing. When this happens, they have reached another level of understanding and will desire more truth and knowledge, and for another opportunity to grow. And at each step of the journey, these new opportunities to learn will be provided. The most important thing is to really live the ideals and love that our religion teaches. We can have the greatest religion of all, but it will not benefit us if we do not put love into practice in our daily living. Whatever we practice becomes a part of us. The group or organization we profess membership to is unimportant; what is important is how we show our love for God by the way we act towards each other.

Heaven is not about religious points of view, but about spiritual actions and love. It is not true, as some people believe that we get to Heaven by giving verbal agreement to a belief in God. We are saved by unselfish love, when we love unselfishly our vibrations become so high that the only location we can fit into is Heaven. We are sorted by the low or high vibrations of our soul so each person lives in the type of Heaven they have built for themselves while living on Earth. Religions are cultural, love and compassion are universal. It is love and spiritual actions, not religious beliefs, which builds spiritual growth. Love is not restricted to any single religion or even religion at all.

All of our faiths have a special role in the awakening of compassion. They all realize the value of love and compassion and have the potential to increase and enhance compassion, harmony, and service. It is on the foundation of these common principles that we can appreciate each other and work together. It does not matter what religion we are. What is truly important is complete love, not religion. Your Religion is where your love is, non-judgmental and unconditional love is the highest form of religion there is.

∽

East Star Edition: *Parts: 1-3*

The **Bible** is: **The Record of a Holy One**. It is preserved, protected, and brought to us by the Creator. The Bible is the symbolic account of the fall and restoration of the human soul to its divine origins. Genesis is the symbolic testimony of humanity's fall from Heaven and paradise lost. Revelation is the symbolic testimony of humanity's restoration to Heaven and paradise found. The Bible should be read spiritually in order to understand it; the Bible becomes inspired and infallible as we open our heart and read it as if through God's eyes. It is not that the book that we are reading is infallible; it is the Creator that lives within our heart that is infallible. When we read it prayerfully, it talks to us; it reveals itself to us. By reading the Bible spiritually and prayerfully, versus literally, the Holy Spirit can guide us the reader, the seeker, into spiritual truth. All knowledge and wisdom comes straight from God.

The meaning of the terms Christ, Christ Consciousness, Christed, Christhood, Mind of Christ, and Christ Force are not strictly to refer to the personality known as Jesus. These terms also refer to the spiritual condition of the highest spiritual attainment possible, the "Ultimate Ideal." We can also label this ideal "Ascension,"" At-one-ment," "Divine-Human unity," "Enlightenment," "God Consciousness," "Nirvana," "Perfection," "Higher-Self" or "Buddha hood" which means Enlightened One, same concept originating in the east; or whatever term we are personally most comfortable with. This Divine-Human unity is everyone's ultimate goal and is spiritually probable for all. All of our souls were created in the beginning and we are finding our way back to where we came from. Jesus became the Christ-Force in that he reached a union of the body and mind with Christ Consciousness -- **Perfect Divine-Human Unity**. It is God's burning desire for all of our souls to reach Divine-Human unity, as did Jesus the Christ, Mohammad, Moses, Buddha, and others.

Our mentality is led by the spirit we are holding, the spirit of God (complete love, divine love, infinite love, non-judgmental love, pure love, *unconditional love, self-love, unselfish love, service,* **UPLIFT,** *unselfish living) or the spirit of the devil-self. People's egos, not the devil, lead them astray. The physical devil that humans fear is a mythological figure we invented that we use to carry the blame for our actions; the real devil is in our own ego and negative thought patterns. The ego leads us astray through self-aggrandizement, self-centeredness, self-conceit, self-condemnation, self-consciousness, self-exaltation, self-glorification, self-gratification, self-indulgence, self-interest, self-promotion, and self-righteousness. The greatest adversary we will ever face is self--the human ego and its selfish desires--this spiritual force of selfishness is the false god we refer to as Satan.* **GOD's mission for Jesus the Christ was to come into the World to teach love and show humanity how Self-Sacrifice and Self-Denial can conquer the ego's selfish desires and how that leads to our full and complete restoration with the Divine Force within us.**

About the Author:

Marzette Henderson Jr. was born and raised in Chicago, IL and currently resides in Chicago's Hyde Park/Kenwood neighborhood with his wife Ayana. He graduated from Western Illinois University with a Bachelors of Science in Law Enforcement Justice Administration. The author has been called to uplift people to be more than what they think they can be through **The Ultimate Inspiration and UPLIFT**. The author is also a Life Coach, Motivational Speaker, and Personal Trainer. He is also a member of the prestigious organization Omega Psi Phi Fraternity Incorporated. He likes to ride motorcycles for fun and is part of the Motorcycle Chapter Envy. Marzette also loves working out and doing community service in his recreational time.

www.ingramcontent.com/pod-product-compliance
Lightning Source LLC
Chambersburg PA
CBHW052158090426
42741CB00010B/2319